Advance Praise for
Fast-Track Your Leadership Career

I am thrilled that Rashim Mogha decided to write *Fast-Track Your Leadership Career*. She has been on various leadership panels hosted by NextPlay and has coached women in tech on how to prepare for leadership roles. She has captured those insights and her real-life examples in this book in the form of a template that can be used by anyone in a leadership role. While most of us seek mentors, very few people put a strategy together for finding a sponsor. Rashim advocates being strategic about identifying sponsors and nurturing those relationships to advance your leadership career. She encourages readers to push the envelope and not be shy to ask sponsors to recommend them for a promotion or a job they are interested in when the time comes.

—Charu Sharma, Founder of Go Against the Flow movement, CEO of NextPlay, Inc., Author of *Go Against the Flow*, TEDX speaker, and a Power Woman. (Charu was listed as a "Power Woman" by Youth Incorporated magazine in March 2012 alongside such notables as Oprah Winfrey, Sonia Gandhi, and Melinda Gates.)

This book is for all emerging leaders. It takes a holistic approach on how to prepare for a leadership role. Today's corporate world is volatile, unpredictable, and ambiguous; it is important that emerging leaders build resilience to be able to manage the corporate stress and lead teams effectively. Vince Lombardi once said, "Leaders are made, they are not born." Leadership is all about exhibiting confidence and decisiveness, and these skills are honed over time through learning and observation. This book dives deep into key focus areas for personal growth and development, and provides great learning through excellent observations and examples. Rashim Mogha is a ferociously dynamic leader with the "make it happen" superpower. She has been instrumental in driving success in various areas in different organizations in the last fifteen-plus years. A firm believer in the power of positivity, Rashim is a thought leader and exactly the right person to write this book. *Fast-Track Your Leadership Career* is certain to give you the foresight and confidence to navigate work issues with ease and fast-track your career to greater leadership heights.

—Amit Chaudhry, Vice President, DataStax

A must-read and reread for aspiring leaders. In this book, Rashim Mogha provides an actionable guide to improve leadership skills, which can be applied worldwide. Her innovative and integrated strategy provides concrete examples of how to build your brand, prepare for a career—not just a job—and network. These are critical aspects of preparing for any leadership role, and you will find yourself coming back to this book again and again for insights. Rashim is a recognized women in tech evangelist, and this book is a result of her passion to give back and prepare a force of emerging women leaders for their next role.

—David Haubert, Mayor of Dublin, Calif., and Founder of Trinity Consulting

A must-read for emerging women leaders. Rashim Mogha's *Fast-Track Your Leadership Career* provides a template on how to prepare for a leadership career. In this book, she weaves in actionable and easy-to-implement advice with real-life experiences that provide a robust framework for leaders. She provides a fresh perspective to leadership by including aspects of mindful leadership and how to lead with compassion.

—Clay Magouyrk, Senior Vice President, Oracle

Fast-Track Your Leadership Career offers great insights and specific practices that Rashim Mogha has applied and tested on her leadership journey, such as acquiring skills required for the next role and finding the right sponsors. It is a guide that emerging leaders need to succeed on their leadership journey.

—Sapnesh Lalla, CEO, NIIT Ltd.

This book provides practical advice on how to take control of your own career and pave your road to leadership positions. *Fast-Track Your Leadership Career* dives into key areas that are critical in one's journey into leadership roles. Rashim Mogha's own story and her career growth demonstrate the power of following these best practices. She covers topics that are real and doesn't shy away from discussing barriers that prevent competent people from reaching their career potential.

—Rana Salman, Leadership Coach and CEO, Salman Consulting

I am so excited to see this practical and sage advice! I wish I had had a template like this to follow earlier in my career. I have found many of the points made in *Fast-Track Your Leadership Career* to be extremely relevant for me. I can attribute much of the growth and success in my career to the implementation of mindful leadership practices and setting healthy boundaries for a better work-life balance. Thanks to Rashim Mogha, you can now learn from the lessons, mistakes, and challenges of those women who have gone before you. This book will help you accelerate your career. Having an actionable guide like this is the difference between having a good idea and taking action to change the world. This book is a must-read for anyone wanting to be a better leader and help manage leaders in their organization. What an impactful resource!

—Noelle LaCharite, Tech Evangelist, Blogger, Cognitive Services Lead at Microsoft

Do you aspire to be recognized as a leader within your organization? Have you been searching for a blueprint that will help you gain the career advancement you deserve? You are holding in your hands a book that spells out the steps that will enable you to reach your goal. In *Fast-Track Your Leadership Career*, Rashim Mogha not only shares her how-to template, but also insightful anecdotes and real-world lessons that led her to leadership positions in well-known technology companies such as Oracle. Open the pages and learn how discovering your "superpower" and cultivating sponsors will fast-track you to your next career milestone.

—Jenny Tsai Smith, Vice President, Startup Ecosystem, Oracle

Rashim Mogha's book, *Fast-Track Your Leadership Career*, provides aspiring leaders a road map for their career journey. Each key area lays out the critical milestones to success in leadership along with the necessary detail and practical knowledge needed to be an authentic and thoughtful leader. This book is for any aspiring leader, as well as those who are already blazing the trail but looking for additional mentoring, coupled with strategies on how to reach their career goals. Many leadership books are too high-level or do not provide the practical advice needed to put theories into practice. The methods provided here can be used immediately and, with continued practice, will yield the best results. Wishing everyone who picks up this book continued success!

—Deanna Kosaraju, Founder/CEO, Global Tech Women

Rashim Mogha is an inspiring leader and her book, *Fast-Track Your Leadership Career*, provides a great tool set for empowering women to start their leadership journey. This book is based on her life experience and includes practical advice. She gives clear next steps on how to identify the superpower that makes each of us unique to excel in the workplace and be happy at the same time.

—Shalini Agarwal, Director of Engineering, Women in tech leader, LinkedIn

Rashim Mogha's wisdom is so fresh, so inspiring. In *Fast-Track Your Leadership Career*, I especially appreciate her empowering focus on "finding your superpower." How many of us really believe we have superpowers? With Rashim's approach, we can all find those superpowers within us. Perhaps the freshest kernel of wisdom comes when Rashim writes about finding a sponsor! Her book mainstreams mindful leadership—a rarity in technology leadership discussions. Last, but certainly not least, Rashim is an example to us all when it comes to building a personal brand. I hope you are as inspired as I was with *Fast-Track Your Leadership Career*. A great perspective on accelerating career transformation.

—Beth Broderson, Group Vice President, Oracle

Fast-Track Your Leadership Career

Rashim Mogha

women lead
P U B L I S H I N G™

Dedication

To my mom, Kamla, who sacrificed her dreams so that *my* dreams could come true.

To my loving husband, Kambiz, who is my rock and has supported me to act on every crazy idea I have had.

To my eight-year-old son, Vivaan, who kept me sane while I was writing this book.

To my six-year-old daughter, Rhea, who aspires to be president of the United States of America.

To my sisters, Shweta and Shilpa, who are inspiring women leaders themselves and are my support system.

To my one-year-old niece, Ravshika, and all young girls who *will* become the women leaders of our future world!

Are you ready to discover your superpower?

Let's get you started on your journey to fast-track your leadership career. Sign up at my website, www.rashimmogha.com, to request a milestone planning template that will help you stay committed to your leadership career goals. I look forward to connecting with you!

Table of Contents

Introduction

I sat there in my office, trying hard not to let the tears roll down my cheeks. I was staring at my computer screen, reading my performance review for the year. Those wonderful words describing my strengths: has a vision, is a strategic partner with strong execution, leads by example, and whatnot. Yet there was one clear message coming through. *"You stay in the same role! You are not getting promoted this year."* I had worked hard, really hard, sometimes putting in almost 80-hour weeks, and I had exceeded all my goals. I went above and beyond to make my numbers, and got raving feedback from stakeholders. But once again, someone else was promoted instead of me. And that someone else *happened* to be a man! I held my tears . . . I didn't want anyone to see me crying in that open-floor-plan office.

I went home and cried my eyes out. I woke up the next day with a knot in my stomach. For someone in her early twenties who had no other passion than work, whose life revolved around work, not getting promoted was a life setback, a tragedy. Luckily it was a Saturday, and I had the weekend to cry and come to terms with the news.

I was a trained project manager. I knew how to navigate ambiguity and find answers. I did that with my clients all the time. So I decided to take control of the situation. I wasn't ready to accept it; I had to fight for what I thought should have been mine—the promotion.

Over the weekend, I read my performance review multiple times to find "opportunities for improvement"—as in why I was not promoted. I couldn't find an answer. So I made a list of questions and a case for my promotion. I planned to meet with the vice president of my organization to discuss why I should be promoted. But as I put this contingency plan together, a little voice inside me told me there was no point in doing so; it was a lost battle. Somewhere in my heart, I knew I was not promoted because I was a woman. Yes, it had happened to me. I had heard from women coworkers how they were passed over for promotion because they were women. But I never thought it would happen to me. I was great at what I did, and I truly believed that if I was good at my job, I would get promoted. Well, *not true!*

I had my meeting with the vice president a week later and, as I had expected, it led nowhere. But it gave me a reason to dive deep to understand what I needed to do to be perceived as a leader and be promoted as one. I had to figure out how to fast-track my leadership career. Because I wasn't taking "no" for an answer.

I firmly believe every problem has a solution, and every solution can be articulated into a plan, a template if you will.

Fast forward fifteen years. I am now a senior director, leading the Customer Enablement charter for Oracle Cloud Infrastructure. I have had a progressive leadership career in high-tech companies, including NIIT, VMware, Amazon, and Oracle. I have managed large teams and built four teams from scratch. I also serve on the Silicon Valley Eastbay Startup Association (SVESA) board and help entrepreneurs build their startup portfolio.

Passionate about seeing more women in leadership positions in the tech industry, I have delivered keynotes and sessions globally, and have been a speaker and on mentoring panels for organizations such as Girl Geek X, Pandora Music, Oracle, LinkedIn, NextPlay, Women Transforming Technologies (WT2), Association for Talent Development (ATD), and PyLadies. My thoughts on leadership, mindfulness, women in technology, and training and certification strategies have appeared in publications including Forbes, ATD, and Thrive Global. I have had the opportunity to teach thousands of people how to be better leaders by building their brand, finding sponsors, and practicing mindful leadership. I thrive when I share my passion with the world. Every time I receive an email from someone who attended one of my sessions and found value in it, it makes my day!

My journey thus far hasn't been easy. It has been a wash, rinse, and repeat process. I have tried and tested what worked and hasn't worked for me and other women leaders, and translated it into a template.

This book is an attempt to share that template with you so you can fast-track your own leadership career. The template is the culmination of more than fifteen years of cumulative experiences, my own and those of many other women leaders who have successfully navigated the corporate environment. I have tweaked, updated, and modified this template over the years to make sure it is lean and current. While this book is written from a woman's perspective, almost everything I talk about in this book can also be used by men to fast-track their careers.

1

My Story

I was born and raised in Delhi, the capital of India. Delhi is truly a cultural melting pot, with people from all ethnicities and religions, Mughal architecture (a blend of Islamic, Indian, and Persian styles), and some of the best educational institutions in India. I am the oldest of three sisters born to a father who is a doctor and a mother who is a homemaker. My mother put her medical career on hold when she found out she was pregnant with me and never went back to it. I was born underweight and was frequently sick as a child. With no support system, my mother put me first and reluctantly let go of her career as a doctor. This was my first exposure to one of the many career sacrifices a woman makes in her life.

Like any other Indian kid growing up in the '90s, I had three career choices: doctor, engineer, or nobody. My parents had just one goal for me—to be a doctor. Their goal became *my* goal. As luck would have it, I fell sick for months when I was in high school and didn't make it to medical school. From this awesome kid on the block who was a role model for many in the family, I was suddenly demoted to a nobody. That was my first exposure to failure, to the feeling of being lost, to not knowing how to move forward. I ended up enrolling in college as a botany major. While in college, my mother—who happens to be my "pillar of strength" and biggest cheerleader—signed me up for a scholarship test for a three-year program in computer science through NIIT. I got the scholarship, joined the program, and my life changed forever. After completing the computer science program, I was offered a job at NIIT, which I happily accepted.

Just when I thought I had finally arrived, life threw another curveball at me. Life is not linear, I discovered. Professional and personal aspirations intertwine. I was not immune. I come from a Rajput family in India, with roots in a royal lineage. And while girls could study and have successful professions, they could rarely have opinions. I had seen my mother and my cousins get married and have no say in decisions. What to wear, whom to talk to, whether to continue with a job or not, when to have children, and how many children to have were not decisions made by the women of the house. I was a living example of the sacrifices my mother had to make. She had to burn her dreams of becoming a doctor to have me. I was not cut out for that life.

The pressure on me to get married started right after I got a job at NIIT. I was in my early twenties. The fact that I was the oldest of the three daughters made it harder for me. My resistance to marriage caused a rift in the family. My father blamed my mother for my audacity. My mother was torn between me and my father. My younger sisters couldn't comprehend my attitude. They didn't understand why I was being so selfish and wouldn't compromise on getting married for the sake of peace in the family. Every evening the atmosphere in our house was stressful and ended with me crying in frustration because my father couldn't see my point of view.

There was incredible pressure from the community too. It became harder for my mother to attend social events because people blamed her for encouraging my audacious behavior. My mother was constantly depressed and couldn't sleep at night. I worked late nights in the office and took on US-based projects to avoid coming home in the evenings; I didn't want to deal with the stress.

One cold night when I reached home, I discovered my father had invited a potential groom and his family to our house to meet me. He had told them that if the boy's family agreed, I was OK with the marriage. I stormed out of the house in anger and kept walking with no intent to return home. I walked about half a mile before I realized I was being followed by two or three men. I was scared. In a country where 106 rapes happen each day and a girl's life is of no value, I knew walking out of the house at night was not the smartest move I could have made. If I wanted to take control of my life, I needed a better solution. I turned around and ran back home.

I knew that to take control of my life, I had to be resilient, financially independent—and away from my house.

The next day I looked at things differently at work. I reviewed the list of senior executives who were managing US-based clients and identified the ones with whom I had some credibility, those who could be my sponsors. I started building my network. NIIT had a significant presence in the US, with an office in Atlanta and many prominent clients such as Microsoft, PeopleSoft, Ford, Sabre, and Sun. I reached out to ask for onsite project management opportunities in the US. I called them to let them know why I was the right person for the job. I told them my superpower—the skills I brought to the table—and what I would do for them. I articulated how it would benefit them to bring me on as an onsite project manager.

I had already worked for some of the clients as an offshore project manager and had delivered for them. Some of those clients had provided great feedback on me, and I had gently guided these clients to send more business our way. Numbers and how my work impacted the bottom line were of importance to these senior executives. They didn't need to know why I wanted to move to another country or what my motivation was. All they needed to know was that if they backed me up for a position, I would be loyal and deliver results.

One of the senior executives I had worked with on various RFIs (Requests for Information) and RFPs (Requests for Proposal), came through for me. He built a case for me to move to the US as an onsite project manager for one of his clients. He worked with the human resources personnel in Atlanta to get me transferred to the US office. That was the start of my personal and professional journey in America. In return, I helped him grow the account, was loyal to him, and ensured that every consultant who came through NIIT at the client site was up to speed and ramped up to deliver stellar results.

I had started building my brand. Over the years, I invested in myself to build my leadership presence and got opportunities to make an impact in various organizations. During my journey, I met various women leaders who shared their experiences with me and helped me grow as a leader. It hasn't been an easy journey, but it has been totally worth the ride.

The valuable lessons I learned from my own experiences and from other women leaders have been instrumental in shaping my successful career as a leader. While NIIT gave me wings to fly and dream *big*, VMware and AWS gave me an opportunity to sharpen my leadership skills. And at Oracle, I found an environment where I can *thrive* as a leader, share my passion, and give back to the community. I have been lucky to work at companies like VMware and Oracle that are committed to bringing more women into leadership roles.

I share my story with you to provide context. When I speak at conferences or other events, I get an opportunity to interact with many emerging women leaders. It is a general perception among them that the women who have been able to "make it big" somehow had it easy or came from premium educational institutons, had a privileged life, or never experienced bumps in the road.

Well, let me bust the myth; that's not true.

Everyone has her own journey, and the path is never easy. Everyone has her share of failures. It is how you deal with those failures and what you learn from them that matters. It is how you respond—rather than react—to those situations that matters.

2

Identifying Your Superpower

I love the word "superpower." It has so much energy in it. Early in my career, when I had successfully completed a high-visibility project, one of the senior executives at my company told my team I had the "make it happen" superpower.

When he said that, I didn't know the term "superpower" existed in the leadership vocabulary. It didn't mean much to me at that time. I was just doing my job. I didn't know what to do with this "make it happen" superpower. How would I activate it, and what could

I use it for? In my world view, superheroes like She-Ra had superpowers.

It took me a few years to understand what "superpower" really meant.

When I talk about superpowers, many emerging leaders ask me how I understood what the "make it happen" superpower meant for me. Here is my response:

I analyzed my work assignments. I noticed I was constantly handed ambiguous, high-priority engagements that called on me to create a solution strategy, then operationalize that solution. While leadership relied on me to deliver successfully, my team relied on me to help them create executable plans. I am a very hands-on person with strong project management skills. They help me manage situations effectively even when risks materialize. To put it in one sentence: I have the power to review the problem, create a solution, and execute it.

Vivian Wong, Oracle group vice president, higher education development, identifies her superpower as collaboration. She says, "I rally the troops. A lot of what we're building is too complex for one person to create. It requires an army to design and develop the product end to end. My superpower helps bring everyone together to collaborate and develop a product or feature that empowers students."

When you think about leadership, various attributes define a leader:

- Strategy and Execution
- Delegation and Empowerment
- Creativity
- Innovation
- Decisiveness
- Empathy
- Integrity
- Inspiration
- Commitment and Passion

All leaders have a combination of these attributes to a varying degree, but one of these attributes is the superpower that sets them apart from others.

As you start preparing for your leadership career, take time to identify and hone your superpower. Why should someone hire you for a leadership position? What do you bring to the table that sets you apart? That's where your superpower comes in handy.

Remember, everyone has a superpower. So how do you go about identifying it?

- ***Ask others:*** The easiest way is to ask others— your managers, your peers, or your clients. You will be surprised by what they have to say. Attributes or qualities that come naturally to you, nothing extraordinary or "super," might be what they consider your superpower. Make a note of what they say.

- **Review situations:** Analyze situations when your peers, managers, and clients appreciated you for something. Make a note of the attributes/qualities they appreciated you for. If you dive deep, you will see a pattern in the qualities people recognize in you. One of those qualities will be your superpower.

- **Analyze your work assignments:** Try and find a pattern in the kind of projects you are assigned. Do they require any special skills? One of those special skills might be your superpower. Even if you don't think the projects require special skills, write down all the skills each project requires. A pattern will emerge. Keep narrowing it down, and you will find your superpower.

- **Identify what makes you happy**: Ask yourself what really makes you happy. For example, some people love to collaborate, others love to problem-solve. In my experience, your superpower is typically tied to what brings you happiness.

Once you go through the process of identifying your superpower, the next step is to hone it. You need to find opportunities within or outside of work to sharpen your superpower. It takes constant practice to polish your superpower.

In my case, after identifying my superpower, I took project management classes to hone my execution skills. To polish the strategy aspect, I got an MBA. To sharpen my skills further, I found opportunities within my company and outside of work to practice these skills. I continue to volunteer in areas where I can use and hone my superpower.

A Woman's Perspective

Women are hesitant to accept appreciation. We downplay our successes, and we are far too humble to take credit for a job well-done. When people express appreciation for an accomplishment, we brush it aside. We are quick to say, "I was just doing my job" or "It was teamwork." We miss an opportunity to identify our superpower in such scenarios.

I encourage you to accept appreciation with grace and take the conversation forward. When someone says, "Thank you for a job well done," ask which of your skills or qualities they found valuable on the project. Dive deep into situations or examples if you can. Each time you ask these questions, you will get closer to identifying your superpower. Identifying your superpower takes practice, and perceptions are always blurry at the start. Don't miss the opportunity to remove the blurriness so you can see your superpower clearly! Once you know your superpower, hone it, and share it with your network with pride.

3

Building Your Brand

Once you know your superpower, the next step is to build your brand. How do you introduce yourself to people? For the longest time, I introduced myself to people like this: Hi, I am Rashim Mogha, <xyz title> from <ABC company>. My role and the company I worked for were my identity. Therefore, my identity changed when I changed jobs.

But there is so much more to me than a job title and the company I work for. Why was I not talking about that? I wasn't sharing a big part of my identity with my audience—I had no personal brand.

I was at a Women in Technology event a few years ago. During the networking session, I met a woman who introduced herself as someone who helps customers make buying decisions. She went on to explain how she did that, infusing her explanation with the values she believed in. In the first five minutes, she told me who *she* was. The introduction was about her, the values she believed in, and how she uses those values to help her customers. That led to an hour-long conversation on customer buying behaviors, our passion about women in tech, and values we believed in. In that conversation, I don't think she ever mentioned the company she worked for or the position she held. She left that to the business card she gave me as we said our goodbyes.

This was a learning lesson for me. Could I hold a conversation for five minutes without mentioning the company I worked for and the position I held? The answer was *no*. So was I really telling people who I was? The answer, again, was *no*. I was telling people all about the company I worked for or my job responsibilities, but I definitely was not telling them who I was. I needed to make sure people knew the real me. I needed to build my brand!

A personal brand sets you apart from others. It is a way to let others know who you are, what you do, and why you do it. It builds congruence between your inner self and your outer self—who you are, where you want to be, and how you are perceived.

So how do you go about creating your personal brand?

Meet with Yourself

To tell people who you are, you first need to discover yourself. Identify and make a list of which values are important to you. Rate them based on your priorities. Then, fine-tune your message around who you are. Not your job title, not your job responsibilities, but how you see yourself. How do your values play into that message? Write it all down. Come back to it again, review it, and make modifications as needed. Discovering yourself is not an easy process. You'll have more than one iteration.

I went through this exercise myself to come up with what defined me. It was a three-step process: 1) identifying my core competency, 2) identifying how it impacts the business, and 3) tying it to my superpower. I noted my core competency as training and certification. My core competency helps drive business through customer, partner, and employee enablement. I use my "make it happen" superpower to create and execute on training strategy to drive adoption of products. Irrespective of my job title, my job responsibilities, or the company I work for, this tagline—"Driving business through enablement"—has stayed consistent. It tells people what I do and how I use my superpower, without tying me to a specific role in a specific company.

Update your LinkedIn Profile

Now that you have discovered yourself, it is time to let others know who you really are. So go ahead: update your LinkedIn and other professional social media profiles. Per LinkedIn, more than 3 million talent professionals actively use the network every day, and more than 200,000 use its recruiting tools to discover and hire talent. So you want to be out there telling people who you are.

Be aware that your LinkedIn profile is more than your resume. Use the summary section to showcase what your business mantra is, how your superpower helps you achieve what you are passionate about, and where you want to be. Now, I am not asking you to share personal details on LinkedIn. When I say "tell who you are," I mean from a business and professional perspective. Avoid putting information about religion, sexual orientation, and political preference on your professional profile.

In the summary section of my Linkedin profile, I focus on what I believe in. Here's what it looks like:

I am passionate about the "Business" side of customer enablement—how it helps drive product adoption and creates a latent sales force of customer evangelists that drives business. My ability to drive executive conversations around training *strategy and vision, and then "make it happen" has helped me drive success for businesses with over $20 million in revenue.*

"There is always a solution and always a plan"…And I lead and inspire my teams to dream big, innovate, learn how to find solutions, and create and execute their plans. The excitement of driving business and customer success through their solutions is a motivator for my teams to perform above and beyond. I am passionate about mindfulness and power of positivity, and the impact it has on an individual's and team's success. I have successfully leveraged mindfulness, networking, mentorship, and sponsorship to build four high-performing teams from scratch and support $20 million-plus training and certification businesses.

Now when people read my LinkedIn profile, they have a better idea of who I am, and the conversation can progress quickly into how I can help them drive their business instead of making them guess who I am.

Write Blogs and Posts

You have discovered yourself, know what your personal brand is, and have put it on your professional profile. What next? Show your personality and your professional acumen by writing blogs or LinkedIn posts. Many people are hesitant to write blogs because they think they are not an expert on the topic. I felt the same for a long time. Sure, I had written books before—but they were all on technical subjects. I had the luxury of explaining what I was saying in more than two hundred pages. How could I explain my point of view effectively in two hundred to four hundred words? I didn't know what people would say or how they would react to my blog posts. What if someone questioned my point of view? I had a good understanding of the business. I could create and execute on a training strategy. But putting my thoughts on training out there on social media was a different story altogether.

I got the confidence to share my thoughts with my LinkedIn network after attending an Association for Talent Development (ATD) conference. I shared my thoughts on enablement with a group of people I met at the conference. One of them reached out to me after the event and said he found value in the discussion and my experiences with developing training strategies. He asked whether I shared my thoughts on a social platform where he could follow me. That made me realize there was an audience interested in my point of view. Since then, I periodically share my thoughts on various platforms, including LinkedIn, ATD, and my personal blog. Many of my posts get linked or referred to in various other posts. It has helped me build my brand. People I don't even know now follow my website or follow me on LinkedIn. By offering their comments and viewpoints on my posts, they broaden my horizon on the subject area. Blogging also has helped me build my network and connect with leaders in the industry.

While you need a fairly good understanding of the subject area, you don't need to be an expert to write a blog or post. Remember that blogs and posts represent your thoughts and opinions. A good way to write blogs is to engage like-minded people by sharing your opinion on a topic and inviting others to comment and share their own views.

Volunteer for Activities and Events

Volunteering for activities and events is a great way to build your personal brand and hone your superpower. If you are from the developer community, you might consider contributing to open-source projects such as GitHub to build your brand. If you are passionate about project management, you can volunteer for Project Management Institute. And if you are passionate about women in tech, you can volunteer for organizations like Girls Who Code. When you volunteer in your area of interest, you give people an opportunity to know you and what you believe in. They see your personal brand in action!

I frequently volunteer for mentoring or speaking opportunities. It gives me an opportunity to meet leaders from inside and outside the industry, and learn from them. It helps me build my brand and be visible among my peers.

Shweta Mogha, senior human resources leader at Amazon, says, "It is important to invest early on in your career to build your personal brand because if you miss out on leadership opportunities early on in your career, it is hard to catch up. The corporate environment is extremely competitive, and people change jobs frequently in order to advance their career. Your personal brand helps you build a reputation within the industry; recruiters reach out to you with job opportunities if you have brand value. However, if the hiring network doesn't know your brand, you are no different than the other hundreds of candidates who apply for the job."

A Woman's Perspective

Women often tell me, "Building my brand requires time and energy, and between managing work and home, I am left with none!" My response to them is, "Outsource what you can." Can your husband or your family take care of the kids for a couple of hours or fix dinner while you volunteer or write your blog post? Can a friend help you review your blog? Can you postpone doing laundry for a couple of days because you have to volunteer today? It is your brand, and you are the best person to create it; so invest in it. Fast-tracking your leadership career requires time and effort. Carve out time for it!

4

Investing
in Yourself

When I didn't get that promotion I really worked for, I was upset, frustrated, angry, plus a plethora of other emotions. But I wasn't going to let "because I am a woman" be my weak spot. I wanted "because I am a woman" to be my strength! I sat down and made a plan for myself. The first action item on that list was to identify what I didn't know. I thought I had everything: the skills, the temperament, and the drive to be promoted to the next role. But clearly, the leadership didn't see it. So how could I make sure, not only that I had these necessary skills, but that people saw those skills in me?

I started on a journey to identify what I didn't know. I spoke to leaders both inside and outside my organization to understand what they look for in an individual they push forward for promotion. I observed the behavior and body language of the leaders. And in the process, I realized I was spending all my weekdays and weekends, energy, and effort on doing my current job, meeting crazy deadlines, and helping my managers meet their numbers. I was giving 200 percent to my current job but doing nothing to prepare for the next job. I was not investing in myself. And while every leader was appreciating me for my ability to "make it happen" and get results, the reality was that they were seeing me as a trusted number two. They saw me as indispensable in my current role, so they didn't want to move me to the next role.

Before I proceed, I want to be clear that I don't mean to say I should not have fulfilled my current job responsibilities because I was focused on prepping for the next job. There will be no next job, no promotion, if you don't do a good job in your current assignment. What I mean is that I was missing out on opportunities to leverage other teams, to delegate, and to reprioritize to make space for personal development.

Emerging leaders need to invest in two areas for personal development: 1) building their functional skills and 2) building their leadership presence. Leaders do not do everything themselves. As one of their functional skills, they identify what can be delegated. Also, when they delegate, they expect you to figure out if you will do that task yourself or delegate it to your team. I had to let go and build time in my schedule to work on my functional skills. I identified key people on my team whom I could rely on and delegated tasks to them. This gave them an opportunity to grow and prove themselves, and gave me an opportunity to work on building my leadership presence.

Work on Your Functional Skills

Functional skills are the skills you need in your leadership role. They are a combination of technical and soft skills. Think about budgeting, project management, people management, engineering processes, and technology as examples of functional skills. You can take classes, shadow people, and practice functional skills. Functional skills are easy to build once you *commit* to doing so. "Commitment" is the key word here. You have to block time in your calendar to invest in yourself to close the skills gap. You need to prepare yourself for the next leadership role. I still block thirty minutes on my calendar every day to learn something new, and that block of time is nonnegotiable. I recently started exercising; so to maximize on the time, I listen to audiobooks while on the treadmill.

Rana Salman, CEO of Salman Consulting, held various executive-level positions before she started her own consultancy company. When she was pregnant with her first child, she was working on her MBA. When she had her second child, she was wrapping up her Ph.D. She says, "There were days when I wanted to give up! But my passion for learning and completing what I started kept me going."

According to her, "As a lifelong learner and someone who enables salespeople to reach their full potential, I believe that investing in yourself is key for emerging leaders. I immigrated to the US at age 11, and I spent most of my teenage years studying. Even though language was a barrier at times, I was raised to not complain and to take control of my own destiny! So, I kept investing in myself and others around me. However, learning and investing in yourself doesn't stop after you get the college degrees. In my late twenties, I was intrigued by sales, and I immersed myself in this career. It was such a humbling experience to get rejected and such an invigorating feeling to win deals and provide solutions to help my customers. Even when I moved into a leadership position, I continued to invest in learning about sales enablement—learned from others around me, read articles, attended conferences, recorded myself, and brutally evaluated my performance after every call."

Rana continues, "My love for learning has led me to dedicate a significant amount of my career to enabling salespeople. I get so much enjoyment out of helping my clients grow. I believe each of us can achieve whatever we set our mind to. However, nothing comes easy, and you must continue to invest in yourself to grow! Surround yourself with people who believe in you, and encourage and challenge you to reach beyond and invest in yourself! It's a win-win for everyone!"

Not just Rana but all leaders I have met emphasize investing in your functional skills while you prepare for the next role. Now that you know why and how to build your functional skills, let's talk about leadership presence.

Master Leadership Presence

Leadership presence is a combination of how you conduct yourself, how you communicate, and how you look. Do you exude the confidence of a leader? Do you communicate like a leader? Do you look the part? Before we proceed and talk about the weight these three aspects carry in constituting leadership presence, let's tackle a sensitive topic.

When I talk about leadership presence at events, I have had some emerging leaders question the "looking the part" attribute. By looking the part, I am not referring to physical attributes. "Looking the part" means "to be perceived suitable for a particular kind of work, position, or role." You have to "look the part" to establish trust and credibility with your audience. Let me give you an example. My father was studying to be a doctor. He was passionate about helping sick people and didn't want to be associated with hospitals that charged a big fee to treat people.

He preferred to set up a private practice where he could decide if he wanted to charge someone or not. In his final year of study, he had an opportunity to speak with a leading physician about how to get his own practice started. The physician looked at him and said, "I would recommend you don't color your hair." My father was self-conscious about his prematurely graying hair, which runs in his family. The physician continued, "When people come to doctors, they are trusting them with their lives. And no one would trust their lives to a doctor who *looked* young and inexperienced. People never trust doctors and lawyers who look young."

My father took that advice, never colored his hair, and went on to have a flourishing practice. His patients trusted him so much they would travel across the country for appointments.

My experience over the years has shown me I do need to look the part to be taken seriously. I specifically remember being in an interview feedback discussion for a candidate being considered for a customer-facing role. The hiring manager had voted "no" on the candidate. When asked why, the hiring manager said, "Did you notice that the candidate had dirty nails, and his hair was unkempt? I never want to put such a person in front of a customer." The candidate was not hired.

To all the women out there, I am not asking you to show up to the office and meetings with tons of makeup and scarlet nail polish. All I am saying is, build your executive presence by dressing like a leader.

Now that we have this sensitive topic out of the way, let's get back to how we develop leadership presence.

Studies show that in terms of leadership presence, how you act (confidence) plays a key role. While most people are confident among a small group of team members or peers, they quickly lose their confidence under stressful conditions. So work on your confidence. Have faith in your ability to pull through a stressful situation. Leaders don't have the answer to every problem. What they do have is the confidence that they can pull the right people together to find the answer. A good way to build your confidence is by looking at all the problems you solved in a week. All those things could have gone wrong but didn't because you were able to intercept them at the right time. Be your authentic self. When you are authentic, you are confident.

Now, let's talk about communication. How you communicate and what you communicate to the leadership team is important. You typically have limited time with them to make an impact. You want to make the most out of it. If you have a meeting scheduled with the leadership team, practice your conversation before you walk into the meeting. Write it down and rehearse it. Also, write down possible questions the team might ask and prepare answers for them. When you are being considered for a leadership role, an opinion is being formed about you based on each interaction you have, so make the best of each interaction.

In one technology company I worked for, Susan was a senior project manager—a diligent and awesome project manager. Her manager, Mary, had worked with Susan for a few years and was considering her for a leadership role. Mary thought it would be a good idea to have Susan present the project's status in the weekly leadership meetings so the leadership team could see Susan's capabilities. After the first meeting, Mary's manager provided feedback to Mary. He said, "Susan speaks very slowly and takes a long time to get to the point." Susan's communication style annoyed the vice president of the business unit. He was impatient and cut Susan off in the meeting. She needed to be coached on how to communicate with the leadership team.

Because Mary had worked with Susan for a few years, she knew Susan's communication style and was OK with it. However, that style didn't work for the leadership team. Mary asked Susan to work on her communication style, and Susan took Mary's advice. She focused on both how and what to communicate to make a positive impression on the leadership team.

Susan also did dry runs with Mary for a few weeks before each status meeting. She was able to showcase her skills to the leadership and change the vice president's perception about her. While Susan had her reasons for talking slowly (she had an Asian accent and wanted to make sure everyone understood what she was saying), her pace of delivery was perceived as lack of assertiveness. Susan took the feedback constructively, improved her communication skills, and was eventually offered a leadership position. I share this story with you because it is important to understand that people's perception about you matters. Others' perception soon becomes our reality.

A Woman's Perspective

While men are prone to overestimate their abilities, too often women lack confidence in their abilities. Exude confidence, and hold onto your confidence in stressful times. Learn how to build and gain credibility with the leadership. Invest in yourself and *do not* sell yourself short!

Rashim Mogha

5

Finding a Sponsor

When I was passed over for promotion—and yes, the job went to a man I thought was far less deserving than me—I spent time figuring out *why* I didn't get the promotion. As I spoke to people, I realized I had put all my eggs in one basket. I had relied only on my manager for that promotion. Then I put all my energy toward exceeding my performance goals. That clearly didn't get me in front of the leadership as someone ready for promotion.

The man who got the promotion barely met his performance goals but invested his time in preparing himself for his next role. He found sponsors and built a network of people who would support his promotion. While I had mentors, he had sponsors. I decided to ditch my mentors and find sponsors. I identified a few senior executives whom I thought were in a position of influence and offered my help on their sales efforts. I had a deep understanding of resourcing, budgeting, and training strategies that was of immense value to the business leaders I approached. And when the time came, I was not shy to ask them for what I wanted.

So what's the difference between mentors and sponsors?

While a mentor is your guide, a sponsor is your cheerleader. To a mentor, you open your heart. You discuss the challenges in your personal and professional life. You share your fears and your apprehensions. And in return, the mentor acts as a sounding board, empathizes with you, and provides you with a different perspective on your situation. A mentor doesn't expect anything from you during the mentoring process.

With a sponsor, you have a different relationship. A sponsor believes in your abilities and pushes you forward. With sponsors, you share your aspirations, where you want to be, and how can they can help you get there. A sponsor is someone who supports your promotion when you are not there in the room and, in turn, expects 100 percent loyalty from you. Because sponsors put their credibility on the line when they back you up, they expect outstanding performance and integrity from you. They want assurance that you will never let them down. As you grow in your professional career, your sponsors can become your mentors, or you can outgrow your sponsors. So it is important to continuously build your pool of sponsors. Finding sponsors is harder than finding mentors.

At any given point in time, you should have three to four sponsors. Be strategic when identifying your sponsors. Not everyone fits the definition of a sponsor. You need someone who is influential and has authority. Your sponsor should be someone with a position of power whom the other leaders trust and value. I would advise you to look outside your immediate circle and a few levels above you to find one. Also, observe the office dynamics. It will help you identify the leaders who hold power and authority.

Once you identify three to four sponsors, the next step is to build credibility with them. In my case, I helped my sponsor respond to RFIs and RFPs for months before I asked him for an onsite project. This was above and beyond my regular job as a project manager. Because I managed project teams for multiple clients, I had a deep understanding of resourcing, development timelines, and our per-hour cost for each resource for those customers—valuable information in responding to those RFPs and RFIs. I had also built professional credibility with my existing clients, so they were happy to give a customer reference if needed.

I was prompt, set the right expectations, and always met deadlines. My sponsor could always count on me. In addition, I also made myself available for calls to explain responses on the RFPs and RFIs if the potential customer wanted to know. This was of huge value to my sponsor, who was a business leader with a sales quota. My sponsor and I both put the customer first and had similar values, so we shared the same work ethic. I had built credibility with my sponsor, and he knew he could rely on me. So when I asked him to consider me for an onsite project manager role, he supported my move.

A Woman's Perspective

We women are hesitant to ask for what we want despite putting a lot of time and effort into helping people. We think we will get our due without telling people what that is. We do our research, assess all the pros and cons of a potential job, and sometimes take a little too long to prepare for and ask for the promotion. I urge you to be strategic in your approach. Identify your sponsors, build credibility by supporting their initiatives, and *don't* be shy about asking for a promotion or a job you are interested in.

6

Practicing Mindful Leadership

The underlying message of mindfulness is being "aware or present." Mindfulness is when the mind is fully attending to what is happening in the moment. In today's world, our lives move at a very fast pace. We pride ourselves on being able to multitask, but the reality is that we live in a continuous state of partial attention.

Being mindful allows us to be present in the moment, to focus on the moment. It helps us move from the state of partial attention toward the state of complete attention, which in turn helps us better focus on the present, think clearly without judgment, and come up with ideas that help our organizations grow and be successful.

Mindful leadership is all about applying the concept of mindfulness to leadership. Practicing mindful leadership helps with:

- **Improved focus** for both the leader and the team, which leads to better employee engagement. According to a Gallup report, approximately 68.5 percent of employees are disengaged at work. Organizations report a 65 percent lower share price over time and 18 percent lower productivity because of disengaged employees! So when you increase focus on the job, it leads to better employee engagement, which in turn positively impacts the bottom line.

- **Improved emotional quotient.** This leads to better communication between teams and groups. When you can understand your emotions, and your reaction and responses to them, you open yourself to understanding others' emotions as well. When leaders have the ability to understand emotions, it is easier for them to drive change and foster collaboration, which facilitates achievement of team goals.

- **Improved resilience.** This helps leaders and teams navigate better in volatile, uncertain, complex, and ambiguous environments.

As an emerging leader, practicing mindfulness not only helps you with productivity but also helps give you the focus and clarity you need to create strategy and vision, and then execute on it. When you demonstrate focus, emotional quotient, and resilience, the senior executives perceive you as a balanced person who can be trusted in a leadership position

So let's talk about how you can be a mindful leader.

Practice Empathy

Empathy is much more than compassion. Empathy is about being able to place yourself in another person's shoes and understand their emotions and feelings. Companies like Amazon and Oracle talk about "customer obsession" being among their leadership principles. How do they practice that? They do that through their employees, who are empathetic to customer needs. Being empathetic helps you better understand your team, stakeholders, leadership team, and customers.

You can practice empathy by being respectful of others, even amid stressful circumstances. Remember, as Carl W. Buehner put it, "They [people] may forget what you said, but they will never forget how you made them feel." Also, give your team, customers, and stakeholders the time and attention they need. Listen to them to understand their point of view. Step into their shoes to understand how things look from their perspective. One of the reasons I had great relationships with my customers and was able to pull in reference favors while responding to RFPs and RFIs was because I empathized with them. I understood their perspective and proposed solutions that they could relate to.

Another way to practice empathy is by showing gratitude and celebrating everyone's victory. We all are busy and, oftentimes, we forget to thank our teams for a job well done! We take their efforts for granted. So make sure to pause and meaningfully thank people for their effort. I have tried this personally, and I have noticed that once I appreciate someone for their effort, others chime in—which creates a wonderful culture of gratitude and appreciation that motivates the team. When senior executives see you driving this culture and contributing to it, they perceive you as a leader.

Women tend to be empathetic leaders. We see our teams as people rather than resources. We can empathize with our team members if they miss deadlines because their child was sick or their parents needed help. At times, it has been hard for me to explain my empathetic leadership style to my leadership team. I have been told not to be overprotective of my team. Hold your ground on that one if you ever face resistance on being an empathetic leader. I have seen women leaders cry when my company had to lay off people to cut costs. They hugged the people who were being laid off, cried with them, and wrote them recommendations. They were empathetic leaders who treated their teams with respect, not just managers for whom the team was simply a resource.

Have a Clear Vision

A vision is limitless and has no bounds. When I didn't get the promotion I wanted, I didn't think about what I did wrong versus what the guy who got the promotion did right. My thought process and plan were all about what I could and should do to get the next promotion. During this process, I also reflected on why I wanted that promotion. Was it just a job title I wanted, or was it more than that? What was my definition of success? And did promotion really mean success to me? Once you identify what success means to you and why you want what you want, you are able to formulate a vision you can explain to people. Your vision reflects your clarity of thought and your ability to communicate that vision to your leaders as well as to your teams.

Assume Positive Intent

As I mentioned before, in today's corporate world, others' perception is your reality. Corporate environments today more than ever are volatile, uncertain, complex, and ambiguous. The corporate politics is real, and it is worse than the *Real Housewives* drama! And while it is easy to get sucked into the drama—don't. Assume that everyone has a positive intent that corresponds to your organization's core values. Give people the benefit of the doubt when situations get tough. When you assume positive intent, you build a culture of trust and positivity, which is important for an organization's success.

Practice a Purposeful Pause

As a leader, it is important to respond rather than react. The decisions leaders have to make are creative; they require resilience and courage. If you work in autopilot mode, in the busyness of the day, the dust never settles. And if the dust never settles, your vision is cloudy and not optimal for making decisions. In my case, I was working eighteen to twenty hours a day managing multiple projects simultaneously. During the day, I was busy running from one meeting to another. In the evenings, I was reviewing everything even after the reviewers had signed off because I wanted all client emails to be perfect, all deliverables to be stellar. I was busy—but was I making the best use of my time as an emerging leader?

I was not giving my creative brain an opportunity to think like a leader. I was just using my operational brain. When I started taking breaks between my calls, I was able to focus better. When I started delegating and letting my team take responsibility, my creative brain found space to think outside of the box for solutions.

Maintain Balance

Congruence is maintaining balance between your inner values and the outer world. In other words, walk the talk. How would you react to an overweight gym instructor who gulps soda while asking you to make healthy life choices? Or a leader who tells you to put customers first when he/she doesn't think about customers while making decisions?

When you work toward congruence, you have a better understanding of your values and an opportunity to model your behavior around those values. So, as an emerging leader, make sure your values and behavior are in sync. This will help you be confident and lead your teams better. When the leadership team sees you as a congruent person, they believe in you and trust you. When there is congruence in values and actions, the path for the entire team becomes clear.

One of my values is to put the customer first. As such, every decision made on a project is based on how it impacts the customers. There have been times when I had to be an advocate for my customers and lock horns with a sales team that wanted to take a different path on pricing or solution. This helped me establish credibility both with my customers and with the leadership team. They knew I was building a partnership with the customer for long-term business rather than short-term gains.

A Woman's Perspective

At mentoring sessions, I often hear from women that they are stuck in a catch-22 when it comes to demonstrating leadership qualities. If they are strong and assertive, they are labeled aggressive and difficult to work with. If they are not assertive enough, they are perceived as too weak to be a leader. I am a strong leader, and I have heard similar feedback about me. When I am called "aggressive," I take a purposeful pause (because my blood boils!) and respond (not react!) to the person. "I am not aggressive," I say, "I am assertive—and there is a difference between the two. Aggression means behavior intended to cause physical or mental harm. It has a negative connotation. Assertiveness, on other hand, means a confident personality, which is a positive leadership trait." I keep correcting people whenever I am called aggressive. Am I tempted to react in these situations? All the time! Do I react in these situations? Mostly no. I pause to respond and not react, and make people aware of their bias.

7

Building Resilience

We live in an overwhelming, overscheduled, and overworked world. Our job roles are continuously changing, and future direction is often muddled by ambiguity. Thus, we are frequently confused and stressed by our corporate life. To cope with and recover from these obstacles, we need to be resilient. Remember—when the going gets tough, the tough get going!

Resilience is one's ability to bounce back, to be able to deal with stress and recover from difficult situations. When I didn't make it into medical school as a teenager, I was depressed for months. I didn't want to get out of bed and go to college anymore. It wasn't because I was lazy; it was because I didn't see a purpose in what I was doing. I had labeled myself a failure and allowed people to call me a failure. While there were many people who pulled me down, my mother was my champion; she told me I was smart and intelligent. She told me I was loved, that this setback should not define who I was as a person.

Everyone's career is a combination of highs and lows. In my career, I have faced many setbacks: promotions I didn't get, projects that didn't go as well as expected, and office politics that I became victim to. These setbacks affected me to varying degrees. I have cried in the workplace, been depressed, and had my confidence shaken. I have had good managers and bad. I myself have been a bad manager at times because of the way these setbacks affected me. A few years ago, I was dragged into particularly bad office politics where I felt like the pawn in a chess game. I was stressed and depressed. When my stress levels started impacting my team negatively, I knew I had to do something. I had to build my resilience so I could cope with the situation and not let it impact my team.

Jenny-Tsai Smith, vice president of Startup Ecosystem at Oracle, shares her story. She says, "Being an immigrant arriving in the United States at the age of 10, with zero knowledge of language and culture, resilience was the superpower I cultivated and relied on 24/7. On our third day after arriving in East Los Angeles, an economically depressed and rough neighborhood, my father enrolled me and my younger brothers in the public elementary school. My first three months in school were challenging, from not knowing how to ask where the restroom was located to fighting off bullies and being in the bottom 50 percent academically (no surprise, as the only subject I could ace was mathematics). I questioned why my parents uprooted us from our comfortable, middle-class existence in Taiwan to a country where I struggled."

"In hindsight, I realize my childhood experience helped me hone my resilience, my ability to bounce back from adversity. Building resilience is similar to building muscles. As you exercise your muscles, you become stronger. Each difficult situation you face head-on, whether with a successful outcome or not, you become more resilient. You don't snap and break; you bend, and then you straighten."

Jenny continues, "My high degree of resilience has served me well in all facets of my life, especially in my career. When I applied for a job at Oracle twenty-five years ago, I was rejected for not being animated enough to be a technical instructor in the education group. It was disheartening. However, I didn't let that get to me, and I didn't give up. When I was invited back a few days later to interview for a technical support position within the same group, I accepted the invitation and was hired. Six months later, I asked for the chance to teach a class. I successfully taught the class and became a technical instructor. A year later, I was tapped to lead a team of fifteen instructors and manage multiple education centers. Since then, things have not gone as planned on several occasions, but my resilience helped me get through those times. I believe that resilience comes from self-awareness and self-confidence. Knowing your own strengths and being confident in your capabilities, you can more readily bounce back from setbacks and turn them into opportunities."

Many of us have been through situations similar to Jenny's. Some people are naturally resilient (think children), while others need to build resilience. So how does one build resilience? Because—let's face it—it is hard when you are in a difficult phase of your life. You can't really shrug it off. Here are some things I have tried to build resilience:

Practice Optimism

The power of positivity is huge. When you are dealing with a stressful or crisis situation in your life, keep reminding yourself that this too shall pass. Remind yourself that you have successfully handled all the hard times you have been through so far, such as failing an exam, breaking up, not getting a job offer, or losing a dear one. Know that you have the power to come out of the tough times by staying positive.

Work on Your Confidence

When hard times hit, the first thing that falters is our confidence. We start doubting our ability to successfully deal with the difficult circumstances. So it is important to keep working on your confidence. Take five minutes each day to list all the successes of your day. You might not think there were any, but when you are stressed and low, even a short "thank you" email from a client or a team member is a success. If you were able to stay calm during a stressful meeting, that's a success. List it! Remember, no success is too small. Optimism leads to success, which in turn leads to increased optimism, which in turn brings more success. It is a cycle, but you need to work toward getting the cycle started.

Ask for Help

Know that you can't do it all. You need the support of your team to keep you up and running in times of distress. So don't be afraid to ask for help. You might need help in terms of emotional support—someone you can talk with who keeps you motivated and boosts your confidence. Someone you can share your feelings with. Or a therapist who can help you navigate your emotions. If you can trust your peers or team members that you manage, get support from them. Make sure you trust any team member 100 percent before you open up to them.

Eliminate Negativity

When the going gets tough, it is natural for the mind to gravitate toward negative thoughts. Make a conscious effort not to let negativity take over. Stay away from negative people or people who find it hard to see the silver lining in a situation. Negative people might bring you down, so it's best to avoid them.

It is OK to set boundaries. Don't hesitate to say "no" to such people and avoid negative conversations. If people come to you to talk about workplace politics, don't contribute to the conversation and gently navigate the conversation to business goals. You do not want to be perceived as someone who contributes to or propagates drama in the workplace. You want to be a leader who can navigate through the politics and keep yourself and everyone focused on the organization's goal.

Be a Problem Solver

Work and success come with challenges. So when times are tough, you want to be a problem solver. You want to think outside of the box and focus on what you, as an individual, can do to make the situation better rather than wait for the leadership to come up with a solution. In 2002-2003 when the economy crashed in the US, corporations were quick to pull back their training budgets. This significantly impacted the company I worked for in India. The leadership tried its best, but people had to be laid off since the US corporations had slashed their training development budgets.

The executive team was looking for out-of-the-box solutions to keep the business afloat in the US while the economy recovered. One of the emerging leaders on our team saw this situation as an opportunity to propose a low-cost solution for her clients. Instead of a heavy graphics and video-based training solution, she proposed a Camtasia-based, low-cost video solution to the customer. In the past, the high-profile clients had always requested high-end, video-based learning solutions. But given their slashed training budgets, they embraced the idea of a low- cost, "quick and dirty" solution to keep their training updated until the economy improved. This emerging leader showed resilience and became a problem solver for the company. She moved on to become one of the executives at the company.

A Woman's Perspective

Research shows that when adversity strikes, women are more resilient than men. When famine struck Ukraine in 1933, young women lived about 50 percent longer than men. However, when it comes to resilience in the workplace, data shows that women are less resilient than men and have high liability scores. According to the resilience diagnostic study done by The Resilience Institute, women are more distressed and vulnerable. So it is clear: when it comes to life skills, women are more resilient than men. However, most women do not build or use their resilience superpower at work. I encourage you to use your resilience at work. When times are tough at work, keep your confidence high, stay optimistic, and be a problem solver. Bounce back!

Rashim Mogha

8

Making Sure
You Are Heard

In my leadership career, many times I have been the only woman with a seat at the table. In meetings where we discussed strategy for the organization, I would put forth an idea, and it would be ignored. A male coworker would rephrase and restate my idea, and suddenly it became a great idea worth pursuing. And I would think, "Wait a minute! That was my idea." Sound familiar?

If you dive deep you will notice that the problem starts long before women enter the workplace. Brothers talk over sisters at home, boys talk over girls at school and on the playground, and that bad behavior is ignored. It is somehow expected the girls will be OK with not being heard or acknowledged for their ideas.

At almost every speaking engagement, women come to me afterward and ask, "How can I ensure that I am heard? How do I make sure my idea is not stolen?" Here are some ways to make sure you are heard, that your ideas are given the attention they deserve, and most importantly, that you get credit for your ideas.

Exhibit Authority

Women and men tend to behave differently in the work environment. While women leaders are generally polite and phrase their conversations carefully so they don't come across as "bossy," men don't shy away from exhibiting authority. That's because most women have been labeled as bossy, aggressive, and stuck up when they exhibited authority. So we are extra careful about how we talk to others. In the process, we often request a favor from people who work for us rather than telling them what do. In my case, when I asked a team member to do a task, I phrased it as: "Can I please request you to do this?" or "Can you please do me a favor and . . . ?" I didn't realize being polite was actually downplaying my authority.

When I share this experience, I am often asked: "So, should we not be polite with the people who work for us?"

My response is: You can be polite while exhibiting authority. Rephrase your sentences. Instead of saying, "Can I please request you to do this?" try saying "Please take this task on." You are still being polite, but now you are exhibiting authority. You are not requesting people who work for you to do their job, you are *telling* them to do their job.

Sometimes you need to make hard decisions in order to set the tone. Early in my career, I had to build a team from scratch for a critical project. The project involved creating about 10,000 pages worth of content on cutting-edge technologies for a large, US-based educational services company. I interviewed hundreds of candidates and selected twenty people for the team. It took about a month to get the team onboarded and ramped up. One of the key requirements of this project was that the content had to be original. The team knew that plagiarism was a deal breaker.

One week into the project, the quality assurance (QA) team informed me it had found plagiarized content in one team member's work. If this content made it to the client, our contract would be in jeopardy. Since this was a high-visibility project, senior leaders of the organization were looped in. I had to make a decision on the next steps. I spoke to the team member about the issue. He confirmed that he had copied content and it wasn't his original work. He had no explanation for his mistake.

I made a decision to let him go immediately and asked security to walk him out of the office. When I informed my manager of my decision, he said, "Are you sure you want to fire him? How about a warning? We are already tight on timelines and losing a resource would not be ideal at this time." I told him I understood that it might impact project timelines, but as a leader, I had to stay firm on the nonnegotiables of the project. If I let this person stay on the team, I would be sending the wrong message to my team. I would set a precedent that people could get away with a warning if they plagiarized.

I kept to my decision, something my manager respected me for as he saw me take charge and establish authority with the team. I called a team meeting and made everyone aware of the issue and of my decision, and we moved on. It was a hard choice for me, but it was important that I set the tone.

Don't Undermine Your Ideas

In an attempt to sound humble and deferential, many women begin their ideas using lead phrases such as, "This is just an idea, but . . ." or "I haven't thought this through yet but . . ." or "I might be wrong, but how about this idea . . . ?" When you start off using such lead phrases, you undermine your idea even before others have heard it. How about trying, "Here's an idea…" or " I want to share this idea." By starting the conversation with confidence, you put the focus on the idea, you give it the attention it deserves, and you alert others to hear you out.

Walk In Prepared

When you get a seat at the table, it is a use-it-or-lose-it opportunity. Make the most out of the opportunity by preparing for the meeting in advance. Learn more about the topic of the meeting before you go. If you have to, practice your presentation or talk in front of the mirror. When you walk into the meeting, stand tall and exude confidence. Contribute to the conversation; be an active participant. Many women are hesitant to share their opinions on a subject outside their expertise. They forget they know enough about the business to contribute successfully to the conversation. They forget the reason they have the seat at the table—they earned it!

As a leader, I have conducted many strategy meetings for my team, and I have noticed that women tend to be passive participants. So I go around the table, asking everyone to share their opinion. As a leader, it is sometimes frustrating for me to see the women on my team agree with everything that was said even when given an opportunity to share their ideas. They forget that if you don't contribute to the conversation, you will lose your seat at the table.

Don't Apologize Unnecessarily

Recently, I was reading an article on how women apologize to save face for other people and how it is perceived as their weakness. As the article went on to explain, the narrative is that women are socialized to be less confident. However, the reality is that they are socialized to sound less confident. It was an interesting perspective and reminded me of a personal experience.

I had a manager who always started a clarifying question on conference calls with, "I am sorry, but I am not sure I understand . . ." She was a smart and confident person, and I knew it wasn't about her lack of understanding. The problem was that the person on the other end was not articulating his opinion clearly. My manager made that person's problem her own problem and apologized for it. In her mind, she was being polite. But others perceived it as a lack of confidence. As a team member, I didn't understand why my manager was always apologizing for no reason. On the other hand, her peer had a different way of handling such conversations. He would say, "That wasn't clear. Can you please repeat the last couple of sentences again?" He was still polite, but he didn't apologize for the other person.

Call It Out

Ever been in situations where you try to say something or share your opinion in a meeting and are cut off by a superior or a peer? It has happened to me multiple times, and left me feeling unheard and unvalued. Now when it happens, I call it out politely. When someone cuts me off, I say, "Wait a minute, I haven't finished yet." When I see dismissal in the body language of the men at the table, I say, "Hear me out before dismissing my opinion." This usually takes the person by surprise and is generally followed by, "Oh, I am sorry, I didn't mean to cut you off." While I would like to give people the benefit of the doubt, I am convinced many of them do it knowingly. By calling it out, I check that behavior. They now know if they try to cut me off, I will call out their behavior. I set a precedent of not allowing people to walk all over me.

Sometimes it is not possible to call people out in meetings. Either it's not the right time, or perhaps you don't want to call your boss out in front of your peers. In such instances, I talk to the individual right after the meeting. I let them know I was not given an opportunity to share my idea. The times I've tried that, my bosses have been receptive to the feedback. It is important that you phrase this conversation carefully; you do not want to be confrontational.

A Woman's Perspective

Yes, I have cried at work! In fact, I have cried many times at work, but not because I am weak. I have cried to let go my frustration at not being heard, of being judged, or being treated unfairly. I want to address this topic because so many women question me about it when I present at conferences and events.

A survey in the book *It's Always Personal: Navigating Emotion in the New Workplace* reveals that 41 percent of women cry at work as compared to 9 percent of men. Crying at work is considered a weakness even though Sheryl Sandberg, Facebook's chief operating officer, has acknowledged crying at work and has advocated for it not to be taboo. What is interesting, though, is that while a woman loses credibility when she cries at work, men tend to be liked for showing their emotional side. I think women are decades away from not being perceived as weak for crying at work.

That won't change until women accept that it is OK to cry at work.

The first few times I cried at work, I was ashamed. I came home and surfed online for "How not to cry at work." But now I think it is OK to cry at work. While my male coworkers pound a fist on the table or curse in anger and frustration, I cry. That's my way of letting go of my frustration.

A few months ago I cried in a meeting with my manager. I was frustrated about my team being played as a pawn in politics between two sponsors, and my leadership's inability to take a stance. My manager's immediate reaction to my crying surprised me. He said, "Don't cry. You are such a strong person." I immediately realized he perceived my crying as a weakness, and I had to address that. I said, "I am not crying because I am weak. I am crying to let go of my frustration about not being heard. Instead of banging on the table and swearing, crying is my coping mechanism. Crying makes me resilient and *not* weak."

The reality is that I am passionate about what I do. I bring my whole self to work, including my emotions. While I try my best to be heard, there are times when I am not. Some situations are beyond my control. Sometimes things are said about me and my team in meetings when I or my sponsors are not there to tell my side of the story. So I am not heard, not treated equally, and my anger and frustration flow in the form of tears. I cry, and then I wipe my tears and bounce back to make an impact on the business.

Rashim Mogha

9

Navigating Through
Work Politics

"I can't deal with this nonsense. How many hours a day do I spend dealing with office politics? It is a waste of my time! I expect people to be adults and work toward a common goal rather than become a rumor mill or play the power game."

Sound familiar? I have said this many times in my career, spanning more than seventeen years. I have thought of throwing down my badge and walking away many times because of work politics. Having worked at four large high-tech companies and with numerous Fortune 500 clients, I now know that politics is omnipresent in every company. Office politics is real, bias is real, and as much as we'd like to avoid getting involved, the fact is that we are all involved in it. Office politics is an integral part of every company's environment.

Office politics exists because people and emotions are involved. The dynamics of limited resources and interdependence of teams make office politics inevitable. I have tried putting my head down and avoiding it altogether, but that is not the best strategy. Because avoiding office politics means I miss out on opportunities for myself and my team. The best way to deal with politics at work is to understand how to navigate and leverage it. So let's talk about how you can do that:

Change Your Mind-Set

For the first few years of my career, my approach to office politics was: I don't want to get involved; I will keep my head down, do my job, and not let it affect me. "Office politics," after all, has negative connotations.

As a result, I didn't invest in building relationships, avoided people I thought were political, and missed out on opportunities to push my projects forward. On the other hand, my coworker was always "connected" and knew what was "really" going on in the organization. This knowledge helped him get stakeholder buy-in and push his projects forward. He called it organizational awareness. I learned from him that it was all about how I looked at politics at work. I had to learn to embrace it and leverage it effectively. When I changed my perspective, I was no longer fighting "office politics." I was using my "office awareness" to make right decisions and rally support for my projects. With this changed perspective, I was more optimistic in my conversations.

Create a Mental Map of the Power Hierarchy

Just like there is an organizational hierarchy based on people's job roles and titles, there also exists an undocumented power hierarchy based on different influencers in the organization. Knowing and understanding the power hierarchy is the first step to organizational awareness.

In the mental map of the power chart you create, you identify who gets along with whom, whose opinion matters, and who can help you rally support for your projects. You will be able to identify some influencers immediately, but others might be behind the scenes.

I often get asked, "How do you know that people whom you are talking to are not backstabbing you or jeopardizing your career?" The reality is: you don't. That knowledge comes with experience. You have to trust your gut and put trust in people. That's why you have to be careful about what you say and to whom. Observe the body language of people in meetings to understand connections and people dynamics. Listen to people, but don't contribute to the conversation by badmouthing others. Over time, you will learn whom to trust. Talk about ideas and business, and not about people.

Distinguish Between Friends and Friendlies

A good way to navigate office politics and not let it impact you personally is by trying to keep emotions out of the equation. You can do so by realizing that not all of the people you talk to at work are your friends. You are friendly with many. You might ask them about their vacation and their kids, but they are not people you would make weekend plans with or hang out with after you leave the company.

Once you realize that most people you work with are your friendlies and not friends, you will be less emotional when you get an unpleasant email from them. After all, it hurts when your friends do not behave as you expect them to.

I am an emotional person and used to take people's comments and actions at work way too personally. Ever since I started making this distinction between friends and friendlies, I have reduced my expectations of my coworkers significantly, and the unpleasant emails don't hurt that much. I can now step back and respond to the emails with facts rather than emotion.

Don't Contribute to the Rumors

In an organization, there are always people who thrive on rumors and gossip. If people come to you and talk about workplace politics, don't contribute to the conversation; gently navigate it toward business goals. You do not want to be perceived as someone who contributes to or propagates the drama at your workplace. You want to be perceived as a leader who knows how to navigate through the politics, and keep yourself and everyone focused on the organization's goal.

Leverage Office Awareness for Impact

The average worker spends two-and-a-half hours dealing with office politics every day, according to Cy Wakeman, author of *No Ego: How Leaders Can Cut the Cost of Workplace Drama, End Entitlement, and Drive Big Results*. If this time is spent effectively to understand influencers and on socializing new ideas, you can make an impact. Going back to my coworker who knew how to leverage office awareness, he leveraged his peers and influencers on other teams to socialize his ideas before he shared them in management meetings. That way he already had buy-in from the power players before he walked into those meetings, and his ideas were approved without resistance since most players were already onboard.

He strategically chose whom to share the ideas with beforehand, depending on who had final approval. He also was careful about how much information he shared, so others couldn't steal his idea. My coworker formed partnerships and leveraged his relationships to positively impact the business.

Follow the Unwritten Rules

Every organization has unwritten rules. These unwritten rules determine how work gets done in an organization. For example, is email a preferred method of communication or is it conference calls? Do your leaders expect you to be available on phone or email after hours? And are there any after hours? Do people respond to emails or do you need to copy their managers in order to get a response?

One aspect of organizational awareness is knowing these rules and following them. In one of the teams I worked with, our manager expected the team to be on instant messenger while we were on calls. It was an unwritten rule we had to follow. Being on instant messenger while on calls helped her get information from us in real time as she was phrasing responses. Also, she could coach us on how to respond when someone asked us a question on the call. It was a big adjustment for many of the team members because we got distracted when she pinged us in the middle of the call to tell us what to say. But slowly we all realized it was a very political environment, and her real-time input helped us navigate the conversation.

Never Go Against Your Manager

This is a cardinal rule. You never go against your manager, unless it is an ethics issue, like sexual harassment or discrimination. I made this mistake once in my career, and the result was painful both personally and professionally. The team I worked with didn't have a conducive environment, and it was getting hard to produce results. When asked for feedback on my manager, I shared some "opportunity for improvement" feedback about him with my second-level manager. Little did I know that what was portrayed to me and other team members as feedback for coaching my manager would be used by human resources and my second-level manager against that manager. I lost credibility with my manager, and he didn't fully trust me even after I shared my intent in providing the feedback. He ended up leaving the organization soon after, and the entire team was a mess. Most of the team—me included—left the organization soon after. I lost a great mentor because I broke the cardinal rule.

It was a sticky situation, and I still wonder what I should have done. Perhaps, when the environment became not conducive to performance, I should have given the feedback directly to my manager instead of providing it to my second-level manager.

Learn to Deflect

When dealing with office politics and sticky situations, not every question requires a yes or no answer. It is important to know that you can respond to a closed question without really answering the question. This is something I have learned over years. Early on in my career, if someone I didn't know asked me questions in an email, I provided inline responses to the email, addressing each question without understanding who was asking the question, why it was being asked, and how my answers would be perceived by the person asking the question.

I was lucky to have a great manager who taught me how to respond to such emails. When she received an email from someone she didn't know, she looked up the person in the internal organization chart to understand the person's role and the context of the email. She analyzed the impact her response would have, then decided how to respond.

Our organization had multiple training and documentation teams aligned to the industry verticals. However, since products overlapped across verticals, the training teams often developed training on the same products, even though the requests came from different verticals. This sometimes caused training teams to step on each other's toes, leading to tension between the teams. One day, my manger received a harsh email from another team's manager asking why some topics that manager's team was working on were covered in our training. The other manager had copied every possible executive on the email.

My manager spent time looking through the organization chart to understand each executive's role and what stake they had in the project before responding to the email. She framed her response so it was all about making a business impact, and how she thought the two teams could collaborate to drive adoption of our products. She became the bigger person in the conversation and showed the execs that she was a strategic leader with the ability to think beyond work politics and join forces with other teams to increase the bottom line.

Know When to Cut Your Losses

There can be times when office politics is overbearing, and there is no congruence between your inner values and the organization. If this happens and the work situation causes you prolonged stress and unhappiness, know that it is time to move on. You always have a choice. And if you have built your brand, invested in up-leveling your skills, and identified your sponsors, you stand a good chance of finding a role in an organization that is a happy place for you. No job, no title, and no organization is more important than your mental, physical, and emotional well-being.

A Woman's Perspective

Bias in the workplace is real. Being a women of color, I have experienced it firsthand. Oftentimes, bias is intertwined with work politics. I have been passed over for promotion in favor of men who were less capable than me. I have been told I should just focus on my job and not worry about a promotion or the fact that I am paid less than my male counterparts. At times I have fought back. Other times, I have leveraged the system by finding influential sponsors to help me champion a project or get a promotion. There have also been times when I decided to cut my losses and move on because office politics was causing too much stress for me. My advice to you is to acknowledge work politics, understand the power dynamics, root for the things you believe in, and stay true to your values. Above all, trust your gut!

10

Learning
to Network

"**B**ut I don't know how to network," I told my
sponsor. "I am an introvert; it takes a lot
for me to get out there and start talking to
people. I can't be friends with people I just met. I find
it impossible to open up in the first meeting. I talk to
people whom I know and am comfortable with."

He replied, "Networking doesn't mean talking to
everyone, and it definitely doesn't mean being friends.
But if you want to grow in the business, you need to
network." This was the conversation I had with my
sponsor after I failed to get a job he had recommended
me for. While he rooted for me, he didn't get much
support from the decision makers because I didn't

have the strong network and visibility in the industry the job required. That was ten years ago.

Since then, I realized that having a strong network is important as you progress in your career. Do you know that for many leadership positions, the right candidate is identified from the employee network even before the job requisition is opened? Do you know that most board positions are not advertised, and the board seats are filled through the executives' network?

Over the years, I have learned how to network and, most importantly, how to put a network strategy in place. It's worked better than just throwing spaghetti on the wall and seeing what sticks.

Practice Networking Everywhere

My husband loves interacting with people and can find something in common with anyone and everyone. I, on the other hand, am an introvert and would rather curl up on my bed with a book. When I started dating my husband, I went to a lot of parties with him. He moved around, talking to everyone within five minutes—and I was lost in the sea of people. He would come looking for me, wanting to introduce me to people, and find me sitting in a corner by myself. When the party was over, he would ask me, "Did you talk to anyone?"

"I didn't know anyone there, and I probably will not see 90 percent of those people again in my life," I would respond. "So what's the point of talking to anyone? I can't just schmooze."

Fast forward to now. I can talk to people at a party without looking for my husband to bail me out of a conversation. I have learned that a simple, "Hello, how are you?" can open a world of possibilities to connect, help each other, and learn new things. All I have to do is to open up and be curious. I am still an introvert and can still get into my shell, but I can snap out of it pretty quickly because I like learning new things and helping people.

Be Strategic About Networking

Networking plays a key role in fulfilling our ambition and being successful. It helps us get our next job, our next client, and our next employee. Therefore, it is important to identify whom you want to network with. About ten years ago, my idea of networking was to go to conferences, collect a bunch of business cards, randomly connect with a few people after the event, and then forget about those people.

Today, my approach is more strategic. Before I go to a conference, I identify whom I want to network with from the business perspective. I read or try to learn about these people before I get to the conference. The first few times I made a conscious effort to network, I just talked about my skill set and my work. I wanted to use those five minutes I had with the speaker or the panelist to tell them how awesome I was. They probably hated me for that! Now at events, I focus on learning more about the people I am networking with, ask them what they are working on, and share my thoughts. In that first meeting, it is more about understanding the other person and finding common interest areas and a possibility to collaborate, rather than getting the job. And then I make sure to keep the connection going.

My friend Rana Salman, CEO of Salman Consulting, calls me a connector. I love connecting people, be it potential business partners or candidates and hiring managers. When I speak at events, I meet a lot of women who are looking for the next role, their next "play." I make an effort to keep a mental note of them. When hiring managers reach out to me for recommendations on candidates, I connect them. It is a wonderful feeling to receive a thank-you note from a person you helped to get a job. The joy and happiness you receive from giving cannot be described in words. It also helps me build credibility in my network; when I need help, I know people will be there for me.

Use Social Media to Network

Social media is a great way to network. Connect with people in your industry on LinkedIn. Many women I speak with are hesitant to connect with people in the industry over social media without having met them in person. I encourage you to make an effort to find and connect with people on LinkedIn or Twitter—people you think will help you grow as an individual, and vice versa. The worst that can happen is you send an invite to someone who does not accept your request. But if you don't ask, you won't know!

About eight years ago, I connected with a training and enablement leader at VMware on LinkedIn. I didn't know her when I sent the request to connect, but we were in the same industry, and I thought we would have experiences and knowledge to share. After a couple of months, I reached out to her to see if there were any openings on her team. When a position opened under her, she reached out to me and encouraged me to apply. That's how I got the job at VMware.

Networking is Not Fostering Friendships

Many women hesitate to go beyond just exchanging business cards or connecting on LinkedIn because they don't consider themselves friends with the connections. Remember that networking doesn't mean fostering friendships. You network with people to help them, share your knowledge with them, recommend them for job opportunities, and expect the same from them for you. To discuss your areas of interest and business values, you don't have to be friends with them. With that said, it does sometimes happen that people whom you network with become your friends over a period of time.

Nurture Your Network

Connecting with people doesn't mean just having them as your connection on LinkedIn. For any relationship to work, you have to nurture it. So take time to follow up with people. Meet them for coffee or lunch, or schedule a monthly 30-minute chat to catch up on each other's worlds. Drop an email or a quick text when you think about a person in your network. If you are in the area, plan a visit. Reach out to them on important events in their lives, like birthdays, holidays, and milestones. Networking is all about giving and taking. When you come across opportunities that will benefit someone in your network, share that opportunity with them. Networking is also about helping people when they need your help. Similarly, when you need help, you should be comfortable asking for help.

Dr. Sherry Hu, CEO of BriteThings, Inc. says, "Learning how to network is critically important for professional growth, since you need resources and connections to be successful. You never know who can help or become your customer in the future."

She consciously makes an effort to meet people, know them, and help them. She says, "I network constantly no matter where I go. I talk to coworkers in the break room and connect with people at social events. I write down their contact information. I have gained tremendously from networking in my own business. I met one of my cofounders in a meet-up group. I also got introduced to one of the major investors in my business by a friend I met a couple of years ago when both of us volunteered to organize a social event together."

A Woman's Perspective

Women network differently than men. For women, networking is deep and emotional. They have fewer but deeper connections. As such, women would rather not network with people unless they can think of or see them as their friends. Most networking opportunities are after work or after a full day of meetings when most women are in a rush to get back home and tend to their family.

I have missed out on networking opportunities at events where I am the only woman leader. Dinner and drinks can become uncomfortable when the men share inside jokes or make sleazy comments without realizing I am there. A couple of years ago, I was at a dinner with a group of male executives when a senior executive made a sleazy comment. Others jumped on the bandwagon to enjoy and contribute to the joke without acknowledging my presence. Knowing that everyone was under the influence of alcohol and there was no advantage to calling the behavior out at that point, I excused myself and returned to my hotel. I missed out on a lot of information shared informally after I left.

So what should you do to make sure you don't miss out on networking opportunities while protecting yourself from uncomfortable or inappropriate get-togethers? My recommendation is to find alternate ways to network. I look for other ways to network with men, such as a one-to-one or a lunch/coffee catchup in a smaller setting, a phone call just to say hello, or an email to share information or opportunities. Effortless networking is an art and requires practice, so make sure you carve out time for it.

11

Building Your Support System

Many people give up on their dreams because they don't have enough time or energy to give what it takes. That's why you need a support system. Having a support system enables you to make career choices and act on them without crumbling under the pressure of doing it all alone.

Often when people talk about a support system, they are discussing a one-dimensional approach that assumes you need a support system in only one area. The focus is either on logistics support for working moms, emotional support to manage work stress, or professional support for emerging leaders. After speaking to many leaders and experiencing it myself, I propose a holistic view to building a support system.

To be able to thrive, we need a support system that includes all aspects of support: logistical, financial, emotional, and intellectual.

Take the example of Dr. Sherry Hu, CEO of BriteThings, Inc. Sherry says, "I have always been strategic about building a support system around me. I realized that I do not know everything in every specific field. I need a panel of experts to advise me when I need to make significant decisions. I also enjoy being on various boards, so it is important to have a well-rounded support system. For my business, I have a board of directors who help me to make important decisions, such as organizational changes and product innovation."

Sherry continues, "For my personal fitness and wellness, I have a group of friends whom I can go hiking, swimming, and dancing with. For my emotional support, I have a handful of close friends I grew up with. We can always rely on each other; safely talk about our life changes, feelings and emotions; and receive honest feedback. For my personal finance planning investments, I have friends who have tremendous knowledge and experience, and we share our investment projects and new opportunities, and learn from each other. I know that my life is happier and richer by having a support system around me."

Sherry has created a holistic support system she can leverage when needed.

When I speak at events, many people ask me how to go about building a support system because their friends are from different fields, have no understanding of how their industry operates, and hence aren't much help when needed. My response is that you need to diversify your portfolio of support. You need different support systems for your different needs. Your family and friends for emotional support; your mentors or network for intellectual support; your financial advisors, bankers, or financial experts for financial support.

So how do you go about building a holistic support system?

Get the Logistics Right

We all have responsibilities beyond work, so it is important to nail the basics and get the logistical support you need. There are just 24 hours in a day, and the challenge is how to fit in our personal and professional commitments in those 24 hours. Who is going to take care of the parents, kids, and/or pets if you take up a high-pressure or traveling job to advance your career?

In my case, I had support from my mother and husband when I decided to pursue my leadership career. I spoke to them and let them know I had a choice: either to grow horizontally or vertically in the corporate world.

My growing into a strong leadership role would need significant support from them. I wanted their buy-in to my decision and to make sure I was being transparent about expectations. I knew there would be times I would have to say no to some of their expectations. My mother and my husband both knew I would not be happy if I didn't pursue my dream, and they were pleased to help out with the logistics. One week before I gave birth to my son, my mother moved in with us permanently and has been there as my support system ever since. With her around, I know my kids get better care than I could give them, and I can pursue my dreams without worrying about them.

I am lucky my mom and my husband could help me out; I recognize not everyone has the family support I have. My friends who can't get support from their family have hired nannies and put a carpool system together for school and other activities. I also believe in outsourcing. I know my time is best spent on my core skill set—my job, speaking engagements, writing books, and running workshops. There are times when I have two or more speaking engagements or workshops a week besides my full-time job. With all this going on, I have to outsource tasks like cleaning the house, mowing the lawn, and getting groceries. I have a team of people to help me get through crazy days. That way, when I am home, I can give my family the quality time they need rather than worry about running the house.

Plan the Money

Often when women think about building a support system, a financial support system doesn't cross their mind. It surprises me that many women have very little understanding of the money being managed by their husbands or fathers. Many decisions pertaining to your career require you to understand whether you have a sound financial standing before you take a risk. So make sure you take the time to understand your finances. Invest money such that you have a passive source of income. When you invest wisely and build your financial support system, you are no longer tied to a job for financial reasons. Hence, when opportunities arise, you can make a holistic decision without focusing only on the money. I have seen many women stuck in jobs because they need the money, even though neither diversity nor their opinions are valued there. Also, financial planning is important so you can build your logistical support system.

Having control of your finances gives you confidence and helps you understand what you are up against when adversity strikes. I have always looked for opportunities to increase my passive income and have a group of like-minded friends with whom I exchange ideas on where to invest. In the last year or so, I have started focusing on financial planning with my friend Sherry's network of financial experts.

Build an Emotional Bank

Bias and work politics are reality in today's corporate world, and no one is immune. Being resilient and having a strong emotional support system help. You want family and friends who can help and support you when you need them. Similarly, you need to be able to support them when they need you. Focus on quality over quantity. Focus on building a *trusted* network of positive people who can uplift you, offer you advice, or just hear you out when you need them.

I have been very lucky to have my mother as my best friend. I can open myself to her, discuss my fears, and know I will never be judged. Even if she can't offer any advice, she will have comforting words for me. My husband is my pillar of support, and the fact that our work industry is the same helps a lot. I don't have many close friends, but the few I have are genuine friends whom I can rely on when I need help. With these people, I have built an emotional bank account.

While most people leverage their emotional bank in times of distress, my emotional support system is also my biggest cheerleader when I have new ideas. My emotional support system is my accountability coach, as well, and makes sure I stick to my plans. My mom, husband, and friends have been there and supported me when I launched my website, kicked off my workshops, and now as I write my book. They have always encouraged my new ventures and gently slipped in words of advice or caution without questioning my decisions. And I have been there for them as well. To hear them out, lift their spirits, and be their cheerleader in their ventures. Remember, it is a bank, so you have to put in before you can take out.

Build an Intellectual Bank

As a leader, you need to be innovative, create strategy, devise out-of-the-box solutions, and make decisions. And for that you need intellectual stimulation. That's why I recommend an intellectual support system. I have a trusted group of advisors and mentors in my network whom I talk with regularly to get ideas on different ways of doing things, to understand their perspective, and to find out how other organizations are solving problems. We learn from each other's experiences and support each other by fostering connections as needed and keep on building the intellectual bank. Having an intellectual support system is the key to growing as an individual and a leader. One way you can build this support system is by networking with leaders in a similar job role as yours. You often meet this group of people at industry-focused events. So next time you are at an event, use tips from the "Building your network" chapter to build up your intellectual support system.

Learn to Say 'No'

One key aspect to building a support system is to build the confidence to say "no." Set right expectations and let your family, friends, coworkers, and managers know there will be times you have to say no to their requests. Let them know you understand there will be times they have competing priorities and have to say no to you too. Saying no doesn't mean you do not care for a person or a task; it just means you have a lot going on and, as much as you would like to say yes, you have to say no.

Women find it very hard to say no. Their natural instinct is to say yes when someone asks them for a favor, and then regret it. If you have trouble saying no to others, change your mind-set. I see saying no to others as saying yes to myself. Because to be able to take care of others, you need to first take care of yourself. If you are empty inside, you can't give anything to others. Once you understand this and change your mind-set, it will be easier to say no when you don't have the bandwidth to help others.

A Woman's Perspective

Women are natural caretakers. We believe in helping others and accommodating requests. But we do not like to acknowledge that we need help too. Building a support system is about acknowledging our need for help. It is about acknowledging that there will be times when we have to say no and that we can't keep everyone happy. So build your support system, and don't rely on the same set of people for all your support needs. Diversify for best results!

12

Your Next
Steps

My story and experiences in this book are not unique. Many of the women leaders I have spoken to have similar stories and experiences. Their journeys haven't been easy, either. Many times in their career, they have been passed over for promotions, have faced conscious and unconscious bias, and have not been heard, just like me. But they didn't let these situations decide their future. They embodied resilience and were determined to succeed. They honed their skills, built their brand, and found strong men and women sponsors who helped them move forward in their careers.

This book is a set of best practices that have helped me become a successful leader. This book is my way of giving back to all the women emerging leaders who are looking for a template to help them get a leadership position and succeed at it. But my writing this book is only the first half of the story; the second half and the end of the story need to be written by you. *This template will work only if it is used.* So I want you to make a commitment to yourself to follow this template and work toward your next leadership role. If you don't commit to taking the next steps, no template in the world can help you achieve what you want.

Be resilient and tap into your support system, but don't give up. Be kind to yourself, hold your head high, continue working toward the goal, and don't give anyone the power to shake your confidence or tell you that you can't get a promotion because you are a woman. When the opportunity arises, go for it! Be confident in your skills, say yes—and then figure out how you will be successful at it.

As next steps:

- Follow my website www.rashimmogha.com for my blogs on leadership, mindfulness, and the power of positivity.

- You can invite me to speak at your next event or conduct a workshop on this topic in your company.

- Set five minutes aside three times a day to meditate and bring your focus back to your goal.

- Carve out some time in the first week of reading this book to identify your superpower.

- Put a strategy in place to invest time in yourself, hone your superpower, and prepare for the next role. I would highly recommend setting aside about 30 minutes each day for learning and to hone your skills.

- Review your LinkedIn profile to reflect your superpower and start building your brand. Spend 30 minutes each month to update your profile as you build your brand. Invest time in writing blogs or sharing articles that reflect your brand messaging.

- Identify ten to fifteen people to network with at conferences, events, or on LinkedIn. Carefully evaluate this set of people you have identified, and focus on five people with whom you will network and build a relationship.

- Create an "influence" map of your organization, and use that information to identify three to five sponsors and build a relationship with them. Let them know you are looking for leadership opportunities, and seek opportunities to help out and showcase your skill set.

I am happy to help and support you on your leadership journey. You can register for an upcoming speaking session or invite me to speak at your next event through my website www.rashimmogha.com.

You can also join me in giving back to the community by recommending or gifting this book to other emerging women leaders.

I would love to hear from you how this book helped you in your leadership journey. You can write to me at rashim@gmail.com.

Wishing you continued success in your journey to a rocking leadership career!

Acknowledgments

This book is a template for fast-tracking your leadership career. While I created the template, the real wisdom comes from my experiences and coaching from various women and men leaders who have been my mentors, sponsors, managers, and advisors during my career at NIIT, VMware, Amazon Web Services, and Oracle. I owe thanks to all of them. In particular, a big thank you to Devenderjit Chaddha (DJ), who was my sponsor and helped me move to the US, and Rochana Golani, my mentor. Without their support, I wouldn't be who I am today.

A heartfelt thank you to Jenny Tsai-Smith, Rana Salman, Vivian Wong, Sherry Hu, and Shweta Mogha for being my support system and sharing their stories in this book. I continue to learn from you each day. I am filled with gratitude for Charu Sharma, Noelle LaCharite, Amit Chaudry, Deanna Kosaraju, David Haubert, Shalini Agarwal, Clay Magouyrk, Sapnesh Lalla, and Beth Broderson for extending their support for this book.

Most importantly, a big thank you to Bethany Kelly, Michelle Bergquist, and Eve Gumpel of Women Lead Publishing for their patience, professionalism, and partnership. Their continued faith in me was instrumental in bringing this book into the world and paying it forward.

Resources/For More Information

I am passionate about empowering leaders to discover, visualize, and actualize their success, and I share my passion with the world through my speaking sessions and workshops on mindful leadership, the power of positivity, and fast-tracking your leadership career. I am available to speak at your next conference or event and inspire your audience to be successful! To contact me, visit my website: www.rashimmogha.com.

You can follow my website to receive my blog posts, and information about my upcoming workshops and speaking engagements. You can subscribe to my YouTube channel "Rashim Mogha," where I regularly upload videos on these topics. You can also follow me on Twitter. My twitter handle is @rmogha.

About the Author

Rashim Mogha is a thought leader who is passionate about empowering leaders to discover, visualize, and actualize their success as leaders.

Rashim specializes in driving customer success through enablement, training, and certification. Her extensive career portfolio consists of prominent companies, such as Oracle, Amazon Web Services (AWS), VMware and NIIT. She has taught thousands of people how to create enablement strategies, harness the power of positivity for success, and practice mindful leadership through keynote speeches, workshops, mentoring panels, power talks, and conferences around the world. Her thoughts on leadership, innovation, women in technology, and training and certification strategies have appeared in publications including Forbes, ATD, and Thrive Global.

Rashim is an evangelist for women in technology. She has been a speaker and served on mentoring panels for organizations such as Girl Geek X, Oracle, LinkedIn, Pandora Music, NextPlay, Women Transforming

Technologies (WT2), Moms Can Code, and PyLadies. She holds a master's degree in business administration in addition to Project Management Professional (PMP) and Certified Scrum Master (CSM) certification. Rashim serves on the Silicon Valley Eastbay Startup Association (SVESA) board and helps entrepreneurs build their startup portfolio.

Rashim lives in Northern California with her husband, Kambiz; her son, Vivaan; daughter, Rhea; and her mother, Kamla. When she is not running around with her kids, Rashim loves to paint and write.

About Women Lead Publishing

Women Lead Publishing is a hybrid publishing company dedicated to serving female authors. Our passion is to give voice, credibility, and influence to authors with a mission and purpose of expanding their thought leadership and impact through published works.

Women Taking Charge Series

The Women Taking Charge series consists of short-read books designed to elevate credibility, influence, and impact for subject matter experts. The series is focused on leadership, business, the workplace, life, and money.

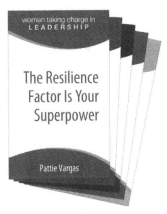

52 Tips Series

The 52 Tips series comprises concise, powerful tips books designed to elevate credibility, influence, and impact for subject matter experts on a variety of subjects or themes.

If you've always dreamed of writing a book and becoming a published author, let us support you and translate your expertise, passion, thoughts, and wisdom into a published book!

Contact us to schedule a no-obligation book discovery session for *your* big book idea!

www.womenleadpublishing.com
800-591-1676

21451507R00066

Made in the USA
San Bernardino, CA
03 January 2019